Green Strawberries

Anna Green

BookLeaf Publishing

Presentation by *BookLeaf Publishing*

Web: www.bookleafpub.com

E-mail: info@bookleafpub.com

ISBN: 9789357445955

First edition 2023

Conspicuous Markers

Conspicuous markers of a painful past invite
questions from curious, well-meaning friends
and acquaintances.

Self-harm scars, a parent who has passed, gaps
in education, always missing class.

A criminal record spent but always lasts, and
four separate primary schools, racked up good
and fast.

Sleeves in the summer? That mark on your arm?
Why so many primary schools, did it do harm?

When did your dad die? How is your mum? And
why, when I mention her, do you look glum?

Now cough up a light-hearted reply
To a question on something you strongly deny
My dad's not dead,
I went to one school,
And never drove teachers right up the wall

Make it digestible, don't share too much. Hide all your pain which is hot to the touch. You can't just start crying, here in this shop, people will think that you've lost the plot. Well maybe I have, for all I know, is that hiding the pain has caused it to grow. In the absence of shame, who might I be? Take a step forward and you might just see.

Motherly Love

Motherly Love
You are safe now, put down your guard
You can relax, although it is hard
You are kind, good, and eternally loving
With so much to give, and so much coming
Open up to the possibility
That staying sad is not how it should be
No need to explain or justify why
It's taken this long to open your eyes
But here you are, sturdy and present
And rejection and abandonment are never pleasant
What happened was real, but can harm you no more
Because you have the tools
To stay grounded on the floor
And at the very least, you are fundamentally fine
With no hidden badness, that you need to hide
Just your humanity, show it with pride
Abandon your fears
And enjoy this life

Shame

Shame is the silent killer
Your cheeks blush pink, your heart rate increases
You compensate for the void within
By looking down your nose at someone else
Who is just living their life, like anybody else
But you cannot bear it
You cannot hide that you hate it so much
Your face feels warm
You look at yourself and all you have done; it all feels so wrong
You compensate for the burning shame
By complaining about how
Your colleague today, made a stupid comment
And it's all on them, and the blame's all theirs
But you are fantastic, like Beyonce or Rihanna
Because you cannot bear
The reality that you feel
That you are innately wrong, and there always will be
And your face burns pink
It let you down again,
Your hands start to shake
And you desperately look at the faces of others for approval or assurance that you are enviably

talented and clever and pretty and worshipped
and revered
When all you need is to know that you matter,
and are loved

Anger

Picked tears
Rise up to the surface
Heart rate rises
Rash decisions
Are suddenly made
Anger is exhausting
That's why I suppress it
No wish to be seen
But grows beneath the light
Shine on your rage
And watch it dissipate
Not fester and bubble
Under the skin, so lift the lid
Release yourself
Swim to safety
Back to land
And after all
I am still me

Remnants

I sit at my dad's oak wood chest
His DNA still embedded
Somewhere in the cracks
I imagine
The clang of bin men
And I relish at the thought
Of even having a bin to change
I can't quite believe my luck

The Truth Can't Hurt

To be told of a morning
By someone unknown
That you sit on a spectrum
And are not alone
You knew all along
But acceptance was slow
Now befriend the truth
You saw long ago

Woman

The Divine Feminine
A circular Mound
Round as a pound
Up in the clouds
We shun our soft midriffs
Resent our red blood
Denied intuitions
Lost deep in the mud
But wisdom is held
In the Roundness of hips
In God's Own Green Earth
Pink, plump pouting lips
In flowing long lashes
Let's fill up our cups
Right to the brim
With a feminine touch

Proof

Proof that I am a woman
Proof I am a witch
Proof that I am good enough
Proof I am a bitch
No authentic response
Comes out of my brain
Just what the people want
And that is my domain

Tight

The tighter you cling
The harder they pull
Away
The very thing you crave
Is the very thing they have
But the way in which you seek it
Makes them hide away

Nonsense

The thought of you
Leaving for more
Brings me joy and pain
In equal measure
For love is not possessive
But it makes you want it all
A painful reminder
That I'm not as I once was
A cheerful truth faced
A double edged sword
Because the truth will set you free
But brings great shame all the same
How to break free
From a shameful truth
Look in the mirror
Breath deeply
Smile
And release

Enya

Dad borrowed the car to go to an Enya concert
But he did not come back
Now whenever I hear her voice
I yell, 'Turn off the track!'
For I cannot see
How Dad came to be
A candle in the wind
Overlooking the Irish sea
I hope he lives the rest of his days
Safe inside Manderley

Counting down

Counting down the seconds
Until I read Rebecca again
Going to order on Amazon
I give it 10/10

Surrender

Art connects you to a higher power
Something flows through you
And you must surrender
But when ego strikes
Your creativity
Falls to the wayside
It's about sales, outcome, approval, likes
Not the process

The Pull

Eyes locked in
A sudden urge
To reply to the messages
You thought were boring
Reaching out to friends, old and new
Lovers you want to forget
For the morning coffee
Is a driver of all things fantastic
But the aftermath bites you on the arse

White Forest

The price we pay for yesterday's sun
Is a foggy, frost-tipped morning
A welcome, white forest
Laid across the land

Inertia

The depletion of joy,
Unfolds with inertia
In direct, inverse correlation
Ego inflation
As compensation
For numbed emotion
Internal commotion

Goggins

As the old adage says
If you're not winning,
You're losing
If you're not growing
You deplete
Wither
Regress
Chug along, roll with the tides
Build every day like Lego
Small pieces forwards
And don't look back

Challenge

I want out of this challenge
Please no more

Interruption

To rudely interject
With a memory, thought or idea
Without waiting your turn
Has the opposite desired effect
Instead of being seen, being heard, and understood
People just stare on bewildered
There's no harm in waiting
You're safe in the queue
Though malice is not
Behind the outbursts
It's a fear of forgetting
That drives going first
An untapped reaction
Without much care
Leads you to trigger
That bewildered stare

www.ingramcontent.com/pod-product-compliance
Lightning Source LLC
Chambersburg PA
CBHW062111140826
49812CB00058B/1307
* 9 7 8 9 3 5 7 4 4 5 9 5 5 *